Old SCOTSTOUN & WHITEIN

by
Sandra Malcolm

This picture shows Whiteinch Bowling Club in Hill (now Edzell) Street. The club was situated just behind where the modern Whiteinch Medical Practice stands in Dumbarton Road, but by 1926 had moved to premises behind the villas in Clydeview, alongside Broomhill Bowling Club.

First published in the United Kingdom, 2003,
by Stenlake Publishing Ltd.
Telephone: 01290 551122
Printed by Cordfall Ltd., Glasgow G21 2QA

ISBN 1 84033 266 2

The publishers regret that they cannot supply
copies of any pictures featured in this book.

The first house in Clydeview was built in 1838 at the corner of Dumbarton Road and Balshagray Avenue. While the roof was being put on it the builders were allowed special leave to go to the celebrations at Glasgow Green for the coronation of Queen Victoria. In the mid-nineteenth century the houses in Clydeview would have had uninterrupted views across the River Clyde and their owners would have been able to shoot snipe in the marshes and reeds on the edges of the river. Owners of these houses were wealthy men, most of whom had businesses in the surrounding area. The manager of Wylie & Lochhead's paperstaining works lived here, alongside Mansel the shipbuilder, a boot and shoe merchant and a retired ship owner merchant. The tenements on the south side of Dumbarton Road (on the right in this picture) were mainly occupied by workers in the local shipyards and when built obscured the views previously enjoyed by the residents of Clydeview. All of the houses in Clydeview were demolished to make way for the Clyde Tunnel and its approach roads.

FURTHER READING

The books listed below were used by the author during her research. None of them is available from Stenlake Publishing. Those interested in finding out more are advised to contact their local bookshop or reference library.

The Last Trains (2) Glasgow & Central Scotland, ed. W. S. Sellar & J. L. l. Stevenson, Moorfoot Publishing, 1980
British Shipbuilding Yards, Volume 2, Clydeside, Norman L. Middlemiss, Shield Publications, 1994
An Illustrated History of Glasgow's Railways, W. A. C. Smith & Paul Anderson, Irwell Press, 1993
The Last Tram, C. A. Oakley, Corporation of the City of Glasgow, 1962
History of Partick, William Greenhorne, John Thomlinson Ltd., 1928
Partick Past & Present, Charles Taylor, William Hodge & Co., 1902
The Story of the Fossil Grove, MacGregor & Walton, Glasgow District Council, 1948
Govan Parish School Board Minutes
This Time of Crisis, Andrew Jeffrey, Mainstream Publishing, 1993
The City That Disappeared, Frank Wordsall, Richard Drew Publishing, 1981
A Nostalgic Look At Glasgow Trams Since 1950, Twidale & Mack, Silver Link Publishing, 1988
Another Nostalgic Look At Glasgow Trams Since 1950, Brian Patton, Silver Link Publishing, 1994
Sure As The Sunrise, Sam McKinstry, John Donald, 1997
100 Years of Glasgow's Amazing Cinemas, Bruce Peter, Polygon, 1996
The Challenge of Need, Lewis L. L. Cameron, St Andrew Press, 1971
The Cinemas of Cinema City, T. Louden, T. Louden, 1983
Notes and Reminiscences Relating to Partick, James Napier, Hugh Hopkins, 1873
Ship-repairing 1818–1933, Barclay Curle & Co., Ed Burrows & Co. Ltd., 1933
The Glasgow Tramcar, Ian Stewart, Scottish Tramway Museum Society, 1983
Yarrow's 1865–1990, Yarrow Shipbuilders Ltd., 1990

ACKNOWLEDGEMENTS

Many thanks to all those people who shared their memories and gave their time and encouragement. To Peter, Rhona and the rest of my family, I owe everything.

The publishers would like to thank Bill Spalding for providing the pictures on pages 30 and 45; Robert Grieves for the pictures on pages 24, 31 and 35; Richard Wiseman for the picture on page 41; and the Scottish Tramway & Transport Society for permission to use the pictures on pages 32 and 46.

INTRODUCTION

Scotstoun and Whiteinch may be small areas, but both have people, places and history of note. Much of their story centres round the lands and houses of Scotstoun estate. A document of 1488 tells of the 'land and tennandrie of Scottistoune' passing from the royal Stuarts into the hands of the Montgomeries of Eglinton. After owning the estate for 200 years, the Montgomeries sold it to John Hutchison, and thereafter it was bought by William Walkinshaw, a merchant in Glasgow. The Walkinshaws were Jacobites and John Walkinshaw, William's son, had to flee in 1715 when the estate was claimed by Alexander, 9th Earl of Eglinton. In 1729 Lord Eglinton sold the estate on to his grandson Alexander, 6th Earl of Galloway, who in turn sold it to William Crawfurd, a Glasgow merchant. Richard and Alexander Oswald, Glasgow merchants whose family came from Caithness, bought the estate in 1748.

The original Scotstoun House, with its Sphinx statues at the entrance, was on the south side of Dumbarton Road just south of Ardsloy Place. It had commanding views across the Clyde, and survived until the late nineteenth century when it was demolished to make way for the Lanarkshire & Dunbartonshire Railway's line between Stobcross and Clydebank. The estate was said to be 'the sweetest seat that sits upon the Clyde' and had beautiful grounds and orchards. Richard and Alexander Oswald were Episcopalians and were generous with their fortunes, giving assistance mainly to educational and religious institutions. Neither man married and on the death of Richard in 1766 the estate passed to their cousin George Oswald. He had seven children, one of whom, Elizabeth, born at Scotstoun in 1767, lived on the estate all her life and died there in 1864. It was she who added a new front to the house in 1825, designed by David Hamilton. She followed the family tradition of carrying out charitable works and it was said that at 90 she had never seen a doctor and at 95 she still retained all her powers of mind and body. When she died in 1864 the estate passed to James Gordon Oswald, the grandson of her sister. On his death his son, James William Gordon Oswald, inherited the estate, although like his father he never lived at Scotstoun. He preferred to travel abroad and when in Scotland spent much of his time at his estate of Aigas in Beauly. Although not resident at Scotstoun, James Oswald still maintained a strong interest in the area. He was a keen evangelist and built Anniesland Hall as a mission hall for the people of the estate, maintaining the property at his own expense until his death at Aigas in August 1937. He and his wife had no children so the Scotstoun estate passed to Lieutenant-Colonel Adrian Gordon Paterson DSO, son of his cousin Alice. One of the conditions of his bequest was that in feuing, selling or letting lands that formed part of the estate there should be a clause prohibiting the sale or traffic in any 'spirituous or fermented liquor': this meant that Whiteinch and Scotstoun were 'dry' well into the late twentieth century.

Whiteinch appears as an island in the River Clyde on Pont's map of 1580–1590 and on Blaue's 1654 map. The name is spelt Whytinche on Pont's map and Whyt Inch on Blaue's, and at this point Whiteinch was an island covered with white sands ('inch' is a Scots word meaning island). At the time the Clyde had a number of islands and was very shallow (in 1769 its depth at high water was a mere three and a half feet and at low water only fourteen inches). As early as 1740 attempts were being made to deepen the channels, and in that year the Clyde Trust arranged with Mr Smith of Jordanhill to spread dredgings from the river over the land on its north side at Whiteinch (including in the channel between the island and the river). In order to hasten the dredging work over 200 jetties were built to assist the river to scour itself. By 1775 vessels drawing six feet of water could sail up the river as far as the Broomielaw, but in 1812, when Bell's famous steamship, the *Comet*, was on her maiden voyage, she was grounded briefly in the shallows at Renfrew.

Whiteinch was still an island as late as 1837, the first house having been built on one of its banks in 1826. Very aptly, it was named Inchbank House, and is still in existence today (situated behind the carpet warehouse at 951 Dumbarton Road). There were almost certainly stepping stones to assist those who wished to cross from the island to the mainland.

In 1852 the Burgh of Partick was created with Whiteinch forming its western boundary. Both Partick and Whiteinch were part of Govan Parish, while Scotstoun belonged to Renfrew Landward Parish. The village of Whiteinch was virtually unknown in 1847, but by 1854 had become a distinct settlement with four streets. The dividing line separating it from Scotstoun was Whiteinch Burn. There were 1,113 people resident in the village in 1858, many of whom were employed in shipbuilding. The first shipbuilding and engineering company to bring industry to Whiteinch was Thomas Wingate & Sons, who set up their works in 1847. Other shipyards followed, as did Wylie & Lochhead's paperstaining works in the early 1860s (paperstaining was an old fashioned method for producing high quality wallpaper).

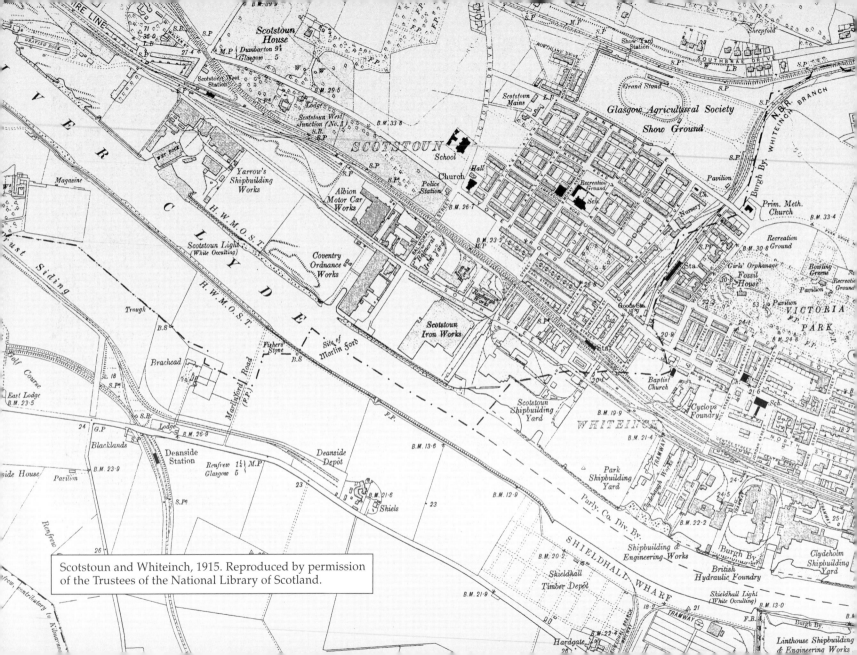

Scotstoun and Whiteinch, 1915. Reproduced by permission of the Trustees of the National Library of Scotland.

In 1895 a housing estate was built along the north side of Dumbarton Road, west of Westland Drive, by the Scotstoun Estate Building Company, with work beginning at Lennox Avenue. The houses between Lennox Avenue and Vancouver Road (Montgomerie Road) were built specially for the gardeners of Scotstoun estate. (Many street names were changed to avoid duplication when Scotstoun was incorporated into Glasgow under the 1926 Boundaries Act.) At the top left of this view is Victoria Drive Public School, and in the centre Scotstoun Primary School and Scotstoun Church. Scotstoun Mains Farm is visible at the junction of Danes Drive and Queen Victoria Drive near the middle of the picture at the top.

Two boys enjoy a quiet stroll along this rural stretch of Dumbarton Road, with the site of the original Scotstoun House on the left and the location of the modern Kingsway flats on the right. The second Scotstoun House (which was replaced by the Kingsway flats) was leased from 1919 by Glasgow Corporation as a home for 'delicate children' at a rent of not more than £120 per annum. In 1962 the children's home was moved to Broomhill and the house was demolished. The hedges lining both sides of the road between Whiteinch and Yoker on Dumbarton Road formed the boundary of the Oswalds' estate for nearly half a mile. This was a very lonely part of the road and on dark winter nights the double hedges were spoken of with fear! Their bad reputation came from an incident in which a ship's carpenter was set upon by two men and one of the would-be robbers was accidentally fatally stabbed with an adze.

The line across this picture of Darnley (now Dunglass) Avenue has been caused by a crack or scratch on the glass plate negative from which it was printed. When the photograph was taken the houses on Danes Drive (foreground) had not yet been built. Houses on the 1895 estate look very similar from the outside, but have varied internal arrangements and features. Some ladies can just be seen at the windows of the house at the corner.

Darnley Avenue, Scotstoun

This picture was taken from the embankment of the Lanarkshire & Dunbartonshire Railway's line, which ran parallel with the river at this point. It looks up Duncan Avenue, with the hill on which Jordanhill House (see page 15) stood in the background and Scotstoun Primary School dominating the middleground. Dumbarton Road is in the foreground, and today this view has been completely obscured by the tenements lining its south side.

The tenements in Dumbarton Road were erected between the 1870s and 1900s to house increasing numbers of shipyard workers employed in large local yards such as Barclay Curle's and Yarrow's. The tall chimney on the left probably belonged to one of the ironworks in the area – the Merlin, Clydeside and Balmoral Iron Companies all had works in the vicinity. It was common for individual terraces of tenements or houses to have their own name and the one on the left, now part of Dumbarton Road, was called Eton Place. The children on the right, standing at the entrance to Duncan Avenue, look quite well-dressed, but the ones on Dumbarton Road have no shoes.

AERIAL VIEW, VICTORIA PARK, WHITEINCH, GLASGOW. A84926 JV

This aerial view shows Victoria Park with its ponds and flower beds. In the background are the earliest houses to be built in Southbrae Drive, and to the left Scotstoun Showgrounds. The picture must have been taken after 1915 – as the red sandstone building of Whiteinch Primary School (now Ladywell School) can be seen at the bottom left-hand corner – but before 1926 as the library does not appear at the corner of Inchlee Street and Victoria Park Drive South. Whiteinch Methodist Church can be made out at the corner of Danes Drive and Westland Drive. The church opened in 1902 and closed in 1981. The original name of Anglegate was restored after the church was closed and sheltered housing was built on the site.

Between 25 and 28 June 1914 the Scottish Aeronautical Society organised a major aviation event at Scotstoun Showgrounds. The two famous aviators at the Scotstoun meeting were Bentfield C. Hucks and Marcus D. Manton. Both men flew Bleriot XI monoplanes: Mr Hucks's had an 80 h.p. engine, while Mr Manton's only generated 50 h.p. Despite complaints from the society that many spectators had taken up vantage points outwith the showgrounds to view the flying displays for free, the event was a financial success. Disappointingly, only a few records were broken, one of which was the Scottish record for altitude flying, achieved when Mr Hucks took his plane to a height of 7,100 feet. At least 12,000 people visited the showgrounds on the Saturday, of whom 1,000 paid two shillings and sixpence for admission to the enclosure, with the remainder opting for basic admission at one shilling. On the Friday afternoon a lucky schoolboy from Glasgow Academy, Allan Muir, won a sweepstake to be taken up in a Bleriot by Mr Hucks. When he returned to the landing arena he said that the ride had been 'ripping'. Other spectators had to pay for the privilege. The *Glasgow Herald* reported that 'Mr Hucks' wonderful flying is the greatest sensation of the age'.

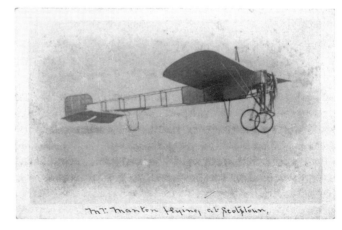

Mr. Manton flying at Scotstoun.

Victoria Park Whiteinch

For many years Partick Burgh had wanted to provide a park for its people, and in 1886 work finally started on Victoria Park. That year there was a depression in the shipbuilding trade, so there were many men looking for employment and the burgh spent nearly £4,000 on wages in connection with creating the park. It was formally opened on 2 July 1887 by Partick's provost, Sir Andrew McLean, after consent was received from Queen Victoria to name it in honour of her golden jubilee. On the evening of the opening day, shops, buildings, houses and streets were illuminated in honour of the event. When it first opened, the park covered an area of about 46 acres, although it was later extended to the north. The main entrance was in Balshagray Avenue and the Good Ladies of Partick (a charitable organisation of ladies of means in the burgh) donated the ornamental gates and pillars there. These gates are now at the entrance on Victoria Park Drive North, where the inscriptions can still be read. The pathways were built to be wide enough to allow carriages to be driven through the park. In 1910 complaints were received about groups of young men being allowed to gather in the park to play cards on a Sunday. The police were called in to take action, but when they appeared the parties dispersed. Undeterred, the police sent in officers dressed in plain clothes, but they couldn't catch the culprits either!

Victoria Park's large pond (seen in the picture on the facing page) measured about four acres in area and was used for the sailing of model yachts and also for skating on in winter. Later, a curling pond was constructed within the park for Partick Curling Club. Another smaller pond was also built to the north of the large pond and it included an island to attract birds to the area. In 1908 a suggestion was put to the burgh that this pond should be turned into a swimming pool, but the idea wasn't taken up. The burgh parks committee agreed to buy three swans from one Mr Bingham in 1906 at a cost of 30 shillings, and in the same year Sir John Stirling Maxwell was thanked for his gift of a young stag to the park.

Partick Burgh was keen to provide a variety of entertainment for its people, and a bandstand, combined with a bowl house and shelter, was opened on 19 May 1908 at a cost of £1,900. The first band to play was the 6th Battalion Highland Light Infantry with pipers. The bandstand had a dome topped with a large crown and stood near the memorial to the *Daphne* disaster. 124 men and apprentices died when the SS *Daphne* capsized at its launch from Alex Stephen & Sons Linthouse yard in July 1883. In 1930 another bandstand was built on the hill beside the flagpole with seating for 2,000. The 90-foot flagpole (which sported a crown at its top) was donated to the park by ex-provost Ferguson, who had been very involved with its purchase and laying out. Another feature of the park is the war memorial, a granite column 27 feet high dedicated to the 1,000 men from Partick who died during the First World War. This was unveiled on 22 November 1922 at a ceremony attended by over 10,000 people. The cost of £2,000 was raised by public subscription. After the Second World War a new inscription was added.

The land on which the park was laid out included Quarry Knowe, where whinstone for repairing roads was quarried. When workers were cutting a roadway through the quarry as the park was being created, they discovered eleven fossil trunks and roots of trees which were over 350 million years old. Fortunately, their geological importance was realised immediately, and a building was erected to protect them from the elements. A temporary structure was put up first of all, but a permanent shelter was opened on New Year's Day 1890. A walkway was erected over the fossils to allow visitors to get a better view of them, and various artefacts were placed on the walls. In 1908 Mr Matthew Hunter, a manager at Alexander Stephen & Sons shipyard (who had served his time as a draughtsman with Barclay Curle & Co. Ltd.) presented a stuffed crocodile to the collection! A Middle Bronze Age cist cemetery was discovered in the layers above the fossils.

Park Drive North from Mound Whiteinch Park.

When Victoria Park was laid out there would have been nothing but fields to its north. Most of the estate visible in this picture was constructed after 1910, although some of the larger villas nearer Westland Drive were built before that.

Jordanhill estate covered 285 acres and, like Scotstoun estate, was in the Parish of Renfrew. The lands of Jordanhill are believed to have originally been owned by the Poor Knights of Christ and the Temple of Solomon at Drumry, but it is known that by 1338 Jordanhill had passed to the Livingstone family. The Crawfurd family became owners of Jordanhill *c*.1542 and remained so for over 200 years. In 1750 they sold the estate to Andrew Houston, who built Jordanhill House, pictured here, between 1782 and 1784. He sold the house and lands to Archibald Smith in 1800, who made additions to the building, as did his son James. When James died in 1867 his son Archibald succeeded him, but only outlived his father by six years. Archibald's son, James Parker Smith, inherited the estate. He was MP for Partick from 1890 to 1906 and was Parliamentary Secretary to Joseph Chamberlain. Several streets in Whiteinch were named after him including James Street, Parker Street, Smith Street, Squire Street, Jordan Street and Hill Street. Buildings belonging to the University of Strathclyde now stand on the site of the house.

The cottages seen here stood at the corner of Anniesland Road and Lincoln Avenue, today a very busy traffic junction. Their site is now occupied by a telephone exchange. Originally this area was part of Windy Edge Farm, which in 1881 covered 100 acres and was farmed by Allan Stirling with help from two men and three girls.

Balshagray estate is first mentioned in 1509 when it formed part of the Great See of Glasgow. In 1641 Balshagray House was built by John Stewart, the last member of that family to be associated with the estate. William Crawfurd of Jordanhill found the house in poor condition but repaired it and added offices and a garden. He also created Balshagray Avenue (illustrated here), the main thoroughfare from Dumbarton Road to the north.

The church on the left of this picture of Balshagray Avenue was built in 1874 as Whiteinch United Presbyterian Church. It was later renamed Victoria Park United Free Church and in 1929 became Victoria Park Parish Church of Scotland. In the early 1960s it was demolished to make way for the approach roads to the Clyde Tunnel. A new church was built at the bottom of Broomhill Drive, but it too was subsequently demolished and houses have been built on its site. Some of the stained glass from the later church was installed in Killermont Parish Church in Bearsden.

There were a number of substantial houses at the top of Balshagray Avenue, one of which, Oswald Villa, was built for the minister of Whiteinch Free Church. Northfield Villa served as the manse for Partick High Free Church.

BALSHAGRAY AVENUE JORDANHILL

There were once two farms at Balshagray: Low Balshagray and High Balshagray. Low Balshagray covered 113 acres and rent of £325 a year was paid during the period 1841–1860 to Miss Oswald of Scotstoun estate. By 1881 the census shows only Balshagray Farm (illustrated here), covering 155 acres and owned by John Fulton, who employed four men and three women.

In 1853 a group of Whiteinch residents held a meeting to discuss the furtherance of education in the area. Until that time children wishing to attend school had to travel to Partick. Mr Wylie of Wylie & Lochhead's paperstaining works agreed to allow the use one of his buildings as a school, and also undertook to canvas and paper it at his own expense, although the committee had to pay to have it floored with wood themselves. Local employers and residents subscribed enough money to pay for a teacher at a salary of £40 per year. This teacher, Mr Fletcher, punished misdemeanours by tying a string with a marrowbone attached to it around the neck of the miscreant, who was made to hop around the room! As the population of Whiteinch continued to increase, moves were made to establish a bigger school, but Mr Smith of Jordanhill intervened and in 1860 the existing school became Whiteinch Sessional School, managed directly by the minister and session of Govan Parish. All teachers employed in the school were required to be members of Govan Parish and had to live in Whiteinch. By the time Govan Parish School Board was formed in 1873, the Sessional School was already overcrowded – in fact a census that year showed that many children of school age were not even attending school. Whiteinch Public School, illustrated here, opened in 1877.

SOMMERVILLE ST, SCOTSTOUN.

At the 1873 census organised by Renfrew Landward Parish School Board, there were 79 children of school age in Scotstoun and of those 50 did not attend school. The following year the board conferred with James Gordon Oswald, the owner of Scotstoun estate, and a school was built in Somerville Street (now Methil Street) at a cost of £2,441 (the ground used as the school's playground is just visible on the left of this picture). It held 120 pupils and was called Scotstoun New Public School. In 1880 a sawmill was built beside the school causing a great deal of noise and dirt, but despite this there were 231 pupils on the roll by 1887.

SCOTSTOUN PUBLIC SCHOOL

By 1895 attendance at the original Scotstoun school had reached 303 and the local school board agreed that a new school should be built. A site at Duncan Avenue was chosen, and the new building illustrated here was opened on 12 April 1901 at a cost of £14,000. As well as teaching reading, writing and arithmetic, the school also provided cookery and science lessons. It was built to accommodate 1,280 pupils, although just before the Second World War there were 1,314 children on the roll.

Victoria Drive Public School, Scotstoun.

Victoria Drive Higher Grade Public School was opened on 31 August 1909 by Sir Charles Renshaw Bart. of Barrochan, chairman of the County Committee on Secondary Education. The three-storey building cost £19,537 and provided accommodation for 1,200 pupils in 23 classrooms. The ground floor was for infants, the first floor for juniors and the second floor for higher grade pupils. An annexe to the school was built in the mid-1930s at the corner of Danes Drive and Queen Victoria Drive, and additional accommodation was added to the rear of the original building in Queen Victoria Drive in the 1960s. During the Second World War a barrage balloon was situated in Raploch Avenue, where part of the school playground was located at the time.

The two short wheelbase model 24 (passenger) buses seen here outside Victoria Drive School in 1928 were built by Albion Motors. In 1903 Albion moved its factory from Finnieston to Scotstoun and continued to prosper there, building new works between 1913 and 1914 in South Street. Albion's contribution to the First World War effort involved the manufacture of 5,594 vehicles, 73,892 shells and an unknown quantity of engines, spares and jigs. Initially Albion had manufactured mainly cars, but from 1913 concentrated solely on commercial vehicles. In 1978 the company employed just under 3,000 workers and in 1987 (having already become part of British Leyland's truck and bus division in 1970) was absorbed by DAF of Netherlands. In 1993 DAF collapsed and American-owned Albion Automotive was established as an independent company.

This photograph shows a typical Albion lorry of the 1920s, fitted with a van body. GB 5317 was a solid-tyred 24 h.p. two-tonner supplied in February 1924 to Glasgow Corporation Tramways Department, where it was used for general collection and delivery work around the several tram depots throughout the city. The photograph was posed prior to delivery outside the main entrance to the Albion offices in South Street.

Barclay Curle & Co. Ltd. moved to Whiteinch in 1855 having established a shipyard at Stobcross in 1818. The company's move to Whiteinch was one of the main reasons for the rapid increase in the population of the area, and by 1860 it employed 950 men. Over the years of its existence (1845–1966) it built 750 vessels, concentrating from 1870 on cargo-passenger ships, mainly for the Indian and Far Eastern services, as well as liners for the Atlantic crossings. In 1912 the company produced the world's first ocean-going twin screw motor ship, the *Jutlandia*.

The 150-ton crane at Barclay Curle's was built in 1919 by William Arrol of Forth Bridge fame, and was known as the Whiteinch Hammerhead. It was the fourth and final Titan crane to be built by Arrol, and was designed to be sufficiently big so that its jib could be swung round over the rear section of the North British Engine Works (also designed by Arrol). A section of the roof was made to slide open to allow the crane to lift marine engines from the works (opened 1914) and deposit them in the machinery space on ships berthed alongside on the Clyde. The vessel in the picture, the *Kenya*, was launched in 1950 and carried 309 passengers. Marine engineering at Whiteinch stopped in the 1960s.

Yarrow's shipbuilding firm had its origins in London, but the high rates and increasing cost of labour and raw materials made a move to Glasgow economically viable, and the company relocated to the city between 1906 and 1908. By opening its new yards at Scotstoun the firm had the advantage of steelworks close by, while the measured mile at Skelmorie was in deep water free from interference and ideal for speed trials of new vessels. Additionally two railway lines ran beside the yards and the river was suitably wide at this point for launching ships. The firm moved from London with most of its machinery and 300 workers, and in contrast to their previous surroundings there were 'green fields everywhere . . . a farm at the back and cows were grazing'.

During the First World War Yarrow's produced 29 destroyers, sixteen gunboats, one submarine, three hospital ships and one floating workshop. The founder of the company, Alfred Fernandez Yarrow, also diversified briefly during the war into the manufacture of artificial limbs made from willow. Materials were in short supply at the time and he advertised the need for willow to provide prosthetic limbs for patients at Erskine Hospital. Truckloads of trees arrived at Scotstoun and one third of the yard's pattern shop was employed in this venture. After both the First and Second World Wars Yarrow's had to concentrate on merchant orders to survive. The noise of the hooters at the start and end of day (and breaks too) was a sound known throughout the neighbourhood.

Most of the tenements along Dumbarton Road were built to house railway and shipyard employees. This view shows Dumbarton Road from James Street (which has now been demolished, as have all the tenements in the picture). Hidden behind the tenements running along the left-hand side of the road are Summerfield Cottages. Mr Thomas Corbett, the father of Lord Rowallan (who was Chief Scout from 1945–1959), erected this row of cottages *c.*1877 with gardens back and front to 'prove that self-contained cottages could pay at a small rental'. The Corbett family was well-known for its philanthropic gestures, particularly in Glasgow. It was Archibald Cameron Corbett, MP for Tradeston (who later inherited the title Lord Rowallan), who gifted the estate and mansion house of Rouken Glen to the citizens of Glasgow. The child on the pavement at the left of the picture looks as if she is suffering from rickets, a common ailment at the start of the twentieth century. Careful inspection of the picture reveals three barbers' poles, with the shops all within sight of each other. For most of the twentieth century no one had any need to go into Partick, far less Glasgow, for shops and services, as every item one might need could be purchased from the numerous shops in Whiteinch. Partick Burgh became part of Glasgow in 1912, and over the following two decades some street names in Whiteinch were changed.

Scotstoun Road, Whiteinch.

69790. JW.

The caption on this postcard reads 'Scotstoun Road, Whiteinch', suggesting it was produced before 1913 when the name was changed to Dumbarton Road. The view looks west from Primrose Street into Scotstoun, with what is now the Scotstoun Emporium on the left. Most of the tall plate glass windows in the first block of tenements belonged to the St George's Co-operative Society. The gap between the two tenement blocks marks the entrance into Scotstoun Street. This was the main thoroughfare for cattle being driven from the wharves on South Street to the goods yard at Whiteinch Victoria Park station (seen middle-right). Many of the children at the right of the picture are barefoot.

Wylie & Lochhead ran an old-fashioned stagecoach between Glasgow and Partick from about 1843, and by 1844 there was a bus every two or three hours. The stables in Partick were moved to Whiteinch in 1850, and the company's buses continued running until the Glasgow & Partick Omnibus Co. was established in 1860. One of their buses can be seen here at the Whiteinch stables. The drivers and guards wore red coats, and the drivers also had tall silver-grey plush hats. William Naismith is the driver in this picture and the guard is George Gilmour. Partick became infamous for being the first place in the Glasgow area to run an omnibus on a Sunday, even although it was introduced for the express purpose of taking people to church! Tickets had to be bought in advance and were not sold on Sundays.

OLD PARTICK, THE LAST 'BUS

Car Terminus, Whiteinch Scotstoun.

Glasgow & Partick Omnibus Co. Ltd. was formed in 1860 and ran horse-drawn buses from Whiteinch to Glasgow. The buses were later replaced by privately owned and operated horse-drawn trams. In 1894 Glasgow Corporation took over the operation of the trams, but it was not until 1902 that the tramways committee decided to extend its network from Glasgow to Yoker, thereby ensuring trams ran through Scotstoun. Trams were able to change tracks in Primrose Street, Scotstoun, just at the district's boundary with Whiteinch, which is where the terminus was located. The tram on the left of this view is sitting at the terminus. To the right is Bowling Green Road. The land at the corner of Westland Drive and Dumbarton Road is now occupied by Victoria Park Bowling Club, opened in 1903.

This accident occurred in May 1931 when tram No. 1123 jumped the points as it turned into Primrose Street from Dumbarton Road, causing it to leave the rails. It had previously stopped at the fare stage at the entrance to Whiteinch Victoria Park station, and was possibly travelling too fast as it approached the corner. The driver, Claude Smith, was inexperienced and had not completed his 30 day probationary period when the accident happened. After mounting the pavement the tram swung round before falling against the window of what is now the Scotstoun Emporium. Claude Smith was killed almost instantly after being pinned below the rear bogey, and rescuers were only able to release his body when the tramways department breakdown gang arrived with jacks to lift the vehicle. Fortunately no one else was injured, even though one man jumped from the top deck in an effort to save himself. The car was finally scrapped in 1960. The Whiteinch Hammerhead (see page 26) belonging to Barclay Curle & Sons can just be seen in the background, as can the signal box for Scotstoun East station.

This Standard double bogie car (No. 1111) is on its way to Dalmuir West and is just about to pass Primrose Street (the site of the accident on the previous page). These double bogie tramcars were designed to give a smoother ride than the single bogie versions, but initially experienced derailment problems on the tightly curved city centre junctions. This made them ideal for long, straight routes, such as that from Auchenshuggle to Dalmuir West. This particular tram was scrapped in December 1960. The small row of shops that fronted the railway goods yard can be seen on the right.

Whiteinch United Free Church originated in 1873 in Jenkin's Cooking Depot at the corner of Squire Street and South Street. Gordon Oswald of Scotstoun estate donated this site at the corner of Victoria Park Street and Dumbarton Road for a permanent church, also giving £500 to the building fund. The halls were opened in 1874 and the church was completed in 1877. Oswald Villa, at the top of Balshagray Avenue, was its first manse. Such was the size of its congregation that in 1900 the church opened a Mission Hall in Fore Street in Scotstoun to meet the needs of people moving into that district. In 1924 the 214th Glasgow Boys' Brigade Company was formed in association with the church, and the company's pipe band was world champion on a number of occasions. After the union between the Church of Scotland and the United Free Church in 1929 a proposal was put forward to rename the building Whiteinch West Church of Scotland, but the congregation decided that Gordon Park Church was more fitting, as that name included a tribute to the man who had been such a generous benefactor to it. Gordon Park Church closed in 1980 when its congregation amalgamated with that of Jordanvale Parish Church, and the building is now used as a bathroom showroom. The tenements beyond Haldane Street were all demolished when the Clyde Tunnel and Clydeside Expressway were being constructed, and the pillar box in the foreground has since been moved round the corner into Victoria Park Street.

Whiteinch Parish Church Mission was opened in 1860 in the Sessional School, but all its members attended Communion in Govan Parish Church, where the congregation was called to worship by the ringing of a handbell. In 1872 the original Whiteinch Parish Church (right) was opened on the site of the present building in Squire Street, but in 1906 the east wall of the church became dangerous and the Partick Burgh Surveyor ordered that it be evacuated immediately. The congregation had to use Whiteinch Lesser Burgh Hall for a year until halls were built next to the condemned church to serve as temporary accommodation. The present building (now housing) was opened in 1913, and in 1929 changed its name to Jordanvale Parish Church, reverting to its original title in 1980 when Gordon Park Church amalgamated with it. When the church closed in 1992 the congregation joined with Scotstoun Parish Church. Whiteinch Riverside station can be glimpsed at the right-hand edge of the picture with Whiteinch Sessional School (now the Orange Halls) on the left.

Whiteinch Baptist Church was formed in 1906 with fourteen members and was initially located in a building on the south side of Dumbarton Road, just opposite Westland Drive. In 1908 the congregation moved into these new premises, built of iron and wood, and by 1910 the church had over 100 members. A new stone church was completed in 1930 with the first service conducted by the Revd W. Vaughan King, minister of Coats Memorial Church in Paisley. The church closed in the 1960s and the final service was taken by the Revd Robert Armstrong, who was also a minister of Coats Memorial Church. For many years the building was hidden behind the Commodore (Odeon) Cinema. It is now used as a furniture showroom.

Dumbarton Road, Whiteinch in 1911. Glasgow Corporation tramcar No. 22 stands at the Whiteinch terminus of the line from Dalmarnock on the east side of the city, which was a red route in the days when the municipal tramway services carried a variety of colour codes for easy identification. This car was one of 120 original corporation horse trams which were converted to electric traction in 1900–01.

Pictured in 1960, Coronation tramcar No. 1274 is seen here on its way towards Partick and just about to pass the Odeon Cinema. This tram was withdrawn from service in 1962 and has been restored to post-1957 condition at the Seashore Trolley Museum in Maine, USA. The site of the Odeon was originally occupied by the Whiteinch Roller Skating Rink. In 1910 a cinema called the Palladium was opened by Scotstoun Palladium Ltd. with seating for 480. It closed in 1924 and Singleton Cinemas opened the Commodore on the site in 1933 after originally drawing up plans to call it the Broadway. Its auditorium seated 2,000 people, and the name and much of the decor reflected the maritime economy of the area. In 1936 George Singleton sold the Commodore to the Odeon chain but by the 1960s cinema attendances had slumped and it closed in 1967. It had a brief existence as a bingo hall, but was demolished in 1976. The Commodore Cafe was located in the block of tenements beside the cinema. On the left of this picture is Victoria Park Bowling Club while on the right are petrol stations operated by BP and Esso.

The hoardings on the left of this picture stood in front of a music hall which was replaced by the Avenue Cinema in 1913. The Avenue belonged to Scotstoun Pictures & Varieties Ltd. and seated 700 people. In 1919 the company sold it and the new owners rebuilt and reopened it in 1930 as the Victoria. A further change of ownership and name took place in 1945 when it was sold to Associated GP Cinemas and became the Victory Theatre. It was rebuilt again in 1949 and bought by the Loray Cinema circuit in 1956, finally closing in 1964. After that it was used as a warehouse for a number of years before being demolished in 1981. Inchbank House, the first house to be built in Whiteinch, stands directly behind a carpet warehouse that replaced the cinema. Opposite the cinema, on the other side of the road, was the Avenue Cafe which sold ice cream and sweets. The tenements on the left-hand side of this picture were all demolished to make way for the Clyde Tunnel. Some of those on the right survive, although many were lost, again for construction of the tunnel. As well as the Commodore and the Avenue, Whiteinch boasted a third cinema, the Premier, which was converted for cinema use from the Victoria Billiard Hall in Dumbarton Road. It was short-lived, opening in 1922 and closing in 1930. In 1905 the speed limit on Dumbarton Road was 12 mph!

WHITEINCH CROSS.

Whiteinch Cross is situated at the junction of Dumbarton Road, Gordon Street (now Glendore Street) and Smith Street. Partick Burgh installed clocks at prominent locations and here a clock can be seen at the top of the building on the left. In 1906 winding the clocks cost the burgh the princely sum of £4 per annum. Most of these tenements on Dumbarton Road were demolished to make way for the tunnel, but proposals for a redevelopment of Whiteinch Cross were unveiled in 2000. An artist was appointed to design a twelve metre high light column to act as a landmark at the Cross, and a clock was set into the wall of the new housing development opposite. Summerfield Brethren Hall was situated just to the south of the Cross.

Whiteinch Lesser Burgh Hall is situated just opposite the park at the corner of Oswald Street (now Inchlee Street) and Victoria Park Drive. The main hall was in Burgh Hall Street in Partick. This smaller venue was opened in 1894 and was used for many purposes: band practice, soirees, magic lantern shows and religious services. The burghers of Partick were very proud of their hall and provided, at a cost of 55 shillings, a handsome uniform for Mr Hamill the hallkeeper: 'a blue serge patrol jacket with 1" mohair braid all round the edge, up back on cuffs and four times across breast, gold tracing braid on collar and gold knots on cuffs, and trousers with 1" mohair braid on side seams'. The hallkeeper's salary was £55 per annum in 1908 and his duties included cleaning, letting, supervising 'rough' cleaning and being in attendance at all lets. Attached to the building was the police station. Initially Whiteinch had only two policemen, but as the population increased so did the need for more police officers. In 1906 the chief constable for Partick increased the force to include one inspector, but by 1908 felt the need to boost the complement to three constables and a second inspector. Additional cells were added in 1906. The burgh used an old ambulance wagon for picking up inebriates and for conveying prisoners from Whiteinch to Partick. The cost of whipping juveniles in 1906 was £1, 4s, 6d per quarter! A fire station also appears on maps of 1895 alongside the police station and hall, and a contemporary account suggests that there were three firemen available for duty. Just across from the hall is Whiteinch Library, opened in 1926.

Taken around 1960, this photograph of Dumbarton Road at Scotstoun shows the row of shops that was built in 1929 just to the west of Queen Victoria (previously Oswald) Drive. Galbraith's Stores are visible at the left, with Scotstoun West Church on the right. In 1900 the Presbytery of Dumbarton feued this site at the corner of Oswald Drive for the building of a church. A temporary iron building was erected and opened for worship in 1901. Work began on a permanent stone church in May 1905 and the first service was held in October 1906. The cost of the new church was £7,300 and the congregation numbered 600. Between 1915 and 1929 the parish, as part of the Presbytery of Dumbarton, extended from the Whiteinch Burn (roughly the line of Westland Drive) to Burnham Road, and from the Clyde well into Knightswood. After 1929 the church was taken under the wing of the Presbytery of Glasgow, at which stage the parish boundaries were changed, making the area it covered smaller. The church's bell was donated by Miss Louisa Gibb and when this tolled on a Sunday latecomers were known to comment that they'd better hurry up as Louisa was calling them! The congregation joined with Scotstoun East Parish Church (originally Scotstoun United Free Church) in the late 1980s and the old church fell into disrepair. It was destroyed by fire on bonfire night in 1997 and subsequently demolished. Flats now stand on its site.

A Standard double bogie tram, No. 1117 (scrapped in 1960), turns into the terminus at Balmoral Street in 1954, while two other cars can be seen in Dumbarton Road (the first of which is Standard No. 58). Scotstoun West Church dominates the background, and there would seem to be a barrier across the south side of Dumbarton Road.

Car 1089 is seen here at the bottom of Anniesland Road in Dumbarton Road in 1960. This single-decker tram was originally built as an experimental high speed vehicle with a separate entrance and exit. In 1932 it was converted to normal use and ran from Clydebank to Duntocher. It was caught on the road during the Clydebank Blitz, but although trapped was spared serious damage. The Clydebank to Duntocher line was closed in 1949, at which point the single-deck trams were replaced by single-deck buses. The tram in the picture was put into storage for two years before re-entering service as a 'shipyard special' with many of its seats removed to allow maximum space for standing. It has been preserved at Glasgow's Museum of Transport.

Until the 1960s and the advent of the Clydeside Expressway, one of the entrances to Victoria Park was at the top of Park Street, on Park Drive South. This picture shows a carriage that may well be about to turn into the park. Whiteinch Primary School can be seen in the distance, while on the right the roofs of tenements in Haldane Street are visible behind the large house on the corner of Park Street.

Park Drive (South) Whiteinch.

The houses in Elm Street (illustrated here), together with those in Park Street, Lime Street and the cottages facing Dumbarton Road, were built between 1888 and 1895 for Gordon Oswald's estate workers. These small self-contained houses with garden plots were considered to be an innovation in social housing and attracted visitors from all over Europe.

43

A view of Victoria Park Gardens (to the right) and Victoria Park Gardens South (left). In the distance is the crane belonging to Barclay Curle and the chimney of Whiteinch baths and swimming pool. These were opened in 1926 as one of the legal requirements of Glasgow's takeover of Partick Burgh in 1912. The steeple on the left belongs to Broomhill (formerly Whiteinch) Congregational Church. Early members of this congregation used the lesser burgh hall at the corner of Victoria Park Drive South and what is now Inchlee Street. The church was opened in 1907, ten years after the congregation had first met.

The School Chapel, St. Paul's, Whiteinch, Glasgow

At the start of the 1880–81 football season, Partick Thistle Football Club had moved to new grounds at Jordanvale Park, the site of what is now St Paul's Whiteinch (pictured above). After complaints about the grounds not being properly enclosed, the club moved briefly to Muir Park (near Partick Burgh Hall). At the end of the 1884–5 season, Partick Thistle moved again, this time to Inchview, where in 1887 8,000 spectators watched the Scottish Cup tie with Rangers, with Partick Thistle winning 2–1. This ground was located beside the north entrance to the Clyde Tunnel and houses have since been built on it. The club moved briefly to Meadowside before taking up residence at Firhill in 1909. St Paul's School was opened in 1905 with 180 pupils, but by 1907 the roll had increased to over 400. The ground floor of the building was used as a primary school and the upper floor served as a church until a new church building was constructed between 1957 and 1960. In 1974 the primary school moved to new premises in Primrose Street.

Whiteinch and Scotstoun were served by two different railway lines. The first to open in 1874 belonged to the Whiteinch Railway Company which constructed a branch from Crow Road to Dumbarton Road. The Whiteinch Tramway Company continued the line across Dumbarton Road and through fields (ultimately the site of Scotstoun Street) to the river. That system came into use in 1872. Cattle was brought from the wharves at the Clyde to the goods yard at Whiteinch Victoria Park station or driven from the yard to the wharves. In 1891 the North British Railway bought the Whiteinch Railway Company, introducing a passenger service in 1897. Passenger services ceased in 1951 and general goods traffic came to an end in May 1965. Houses in Westland Drive can be seen just behind the locomotive in this picture, taken just north of Whiteinch Victoria Park station. In 1934, 50 Canadian bullocks stampeded from Merkland's Wharf and caused chaos in the area for quite some time. A train at Jordanhill station had to be delayed while cattle were removed from the line, and visitors to Victoria Park were entertained by the sight of a number of beasts paddling in the pond there. Allotments in Scotstoun were trampled on and a football match being played on a pitch beside Crow Road had to be delayed until the drovers could round up the animals. The ground occupied by the former railway is now part of a nature walk leading from Dumbarton Road to Crow Road.

In 1896 the Lanarkshire & Dunbartonshire Railway's new line provided a link between Stobcross and Clydebank, with three stations in the area: Whiteinch Riverside, Scotstoun East and Scotstoun West. This 1962 picture of Scotstoun East station shows a Fairburn LMS Class 4MT 2-6-4 tank engine, which was built at Derby works in 1948 and withdrawn in February 1966. Cairns Dairies' corner shop in Scotstoun Street is just hidden behind the front of the locomotive. Passenger services on the line were withdrawn in 1964 and the trackbed ultimately became part of the Glasgow to Loch Lomond cycleway.

The Salvation Army's original halls (now demolished) were in Parker Street. Permission to build them had been applied for in 1914. One of the commemorative stones was laid by James Parker Smith of Jordanhill who was MP for Partick. When the halls were demolished the Citadel moved to new premises in Medwyn Street. The band members in this 1923 photograph are (left to right):

Back row: C. Allison, C. Pithkeatly, S. Mackenzie, G. Pocock, H. Sandford, H. Calder, J. Kennedy, W. Calder

Middle row: W. Gordon, G. Kerr, J. Culpeck, R. Innes, J. King, J. J. Frazer, W. Calder, J. Galbraith, W. Knight, D. H. Green, J. Gordon

Front row: B. Green, C. Singleton, J. Robertson, T. Stewart, W. Greer, W. Mackenzie, R. Mackenzie, R. Duff, G. English, W. McConnell